cont

CW00376306

British & North American Readers:
Please note that Australian cup and
spoon measurements are metric. A quick
conversion guide appears on page 63.
A glossary explaining unfamiliar terms
and ingredients begins on page 60.

# for starters

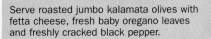

Barbecue thick slices of haloumi cheese; serve drizzled with freshly squeezed lemon or lime juice, topped with chopped fresh flat-leaf parsley.

Serve crisp oven-baked tortilla wedges with a salsa of avocado, tomato, lime juice, coriander and red onion.

Combine bottled pesto with light sour cream and serve, with crudités, as a delicious dip.

Serve roasted jumbo kalamata olives with fetta cheese, fresh baby oregano leaves and freshly cracked black pepper.

Top freshly shucked oysters with a squeeze of lime juice, a drizzle of kecap manis, lime zest shreds and shredded pickled ginger.

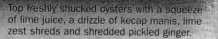
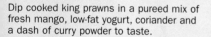

Dip cooked king prawns in a pureed mix of fresh mango, low-fat yogurt, coriander and a dash of curry powder to taste.

Serve crumbled grilled prosciutto over steamed asparagus, drizzled with extra virgin olive oil; top with parmesan cheese flakes.

Drizzle roasted potato wedges with a mixutre of crème fraîche and chopped chives; top with sliced green onions, smoked salmon slices and a spoonful of salmon roe.

4 **prawn** and
mint salad

1kg medium cooked prawns

1 lebanese cucumber (130g)

1 tablespoon fish sauce

1/4 cup (60ml) lime juice

1/2 cup (125ml) coconut milk

2 tablespoons sugar

1 clove garlic, crushed

2 teaspoons grated fresh ginger

1 fresh red thai chilli, seeded, sliced thinly

60g snow pea tendrils

3 cups (60g) watercress

2 cups (160g) bean sprouts

1/2 cup shredded fresh mint

Shell and devein prawns,
leaving tails intact.
Halve cucumber lengthways,
slice thinly on the diagonal.
Whisk sauce, juice, milk, sugar,
garlic, ginger and chilli in large
bowl; add prawns, cucumber
and remaining ingredients,
toss salad gently to combine.

SERVES 4
per serving 8.7g fat; 1087kJ
on the table in 30 minutes

6 bucatini with

baked ricotta

2 x 270g jars
marinated eggplant
in oil

2 cloves garlic,
crushed

375g bucatini

2 x 400g cans
tomatoes

1/2 teaspoon cracked
black pepper

300g baked ricotta,
chopped coarsely

Cook undrained eggplant and garlic in large saucepan, stirring, until fragrant.
Meanwhile, cook pasta in large saucepan of boiling water, uncovered, until just tender; drain.
Stir pasta, undrained crushed tomatoes and pepper into eggplant mixture; toss over medium heat until combined, then gently stir in ricotta.

SERVES 4
per serving 32.4g fat; 3352kJ
on the table in 20 minutes

satay beef stir-fry
with hokkien noodles

600g hokkien noodles

300g beef rump steak, sliced thinly

1/2 teaspoon grated fresh ginger

2 teaspoons sesame oil

1 small red onion (100g), sliced thinly

1 medium red capsicum (200g), sliced thinly

2 teaspoons lime juice

1/4 cup (75g) satay sauce

1 tablespoon hoisin sauce

1/3 cup (80ml) soy sauce

1 tablespoon kecap manis

150g snow peas

1 tablespoon finely chopped fresh coriander

1/4 cup (35g) unsalted roasted peanuts, chopped coarsely

Rinse noodles under hot water; drain. Transfer to large bowl; separate noodles with fork.
Heat oiled wok or large non-stick frying pan; stir-fry beef and ginger until beef is browned, remove from wok.
Heat oil in wok; stir-fry onion and capsicum until just tender. Return beef mixture to wok with combined juice and sauces; stir-fry until sauce boils. Add noodles and snow peas; stir-fry until hot. Add coriander, serve sprinkled with peanuts.

SERVES 4
per serving 21.4g fat; 2131kJ
on the table in 30 minutes

fettuccine with summer
tomato sauce

375g fettuccine

2 large tomatoes (500g), chopped finely

1 medium white onion (150g),
chopped finely

6 seeded green olives, chopped finely

1 tablespoon capers, drained,
chopped finely

2 teaspoons finely chopped
fresh oregano

1/3 cup finely chopped fresh
flat-leaf parsley

2 cloves garlic, crushed

1/4 cup (60ml) olive oil

Cook pasta in large saucepan of
boiling water, uncovered, until tender.
Meanwhile, combine remaining
ingredients in large bowl; mix well.
Toss drained pasta with tomato mixture.

SERVES 4
per serving 15g fat; 1979kJ
on the table in 20 minutes

ginger **pork** stir-fry

700g pork fillets,
sliced thinly

2 tablespoons grated
fresh ginger

1/4 cup finely chopped
fresh coriander

2 tablespoons
peanut oil

1 medium white onion
(150g), sliced thinly

1 medium yellow
capsicum (200g),
sliced thinly

1 medium red
capsicum (200g),
sliced thinly

2 tablespoons light
soy sauce

2 tablespoons
rice vinegar

3 cups (240g)
bean sprouts

Combine pork, ginger and coriander in
medium bowl.

Heat oil in wok or large frying pan; stir-fry
pork mixture and onion, in batches, until
pork is browned and cooked through.

Stir-fry capsicums in wok until just tender
and browned lightly. Return pork mixture
to wok; stir in soy sauce and vinegar.
Add sprouts; stir-fry until hot.

SERVES 4
per serving 13.4g fat; 1342kJ
on the table in 35 minutes

crisp green
vegetables with tempeh

Fresh tofu may be used in place of the tempeh, if desired.

1 tablespoon peanut oil

300g tempeh, chopped finely

1 medium brown onion (150g), sliced thinly

3 cloves garlic, crushed

500g fresh asparagus, halved lengthways

200g sugar snap peas

200g baby bok choy, halved

2¹/₂ cups (200g) bean sprouts

¹/₄ cup (60ml) soy sauce

¹/₄ cup (60ml) vegetable stock

¹/₄ cup (60ml) mirin

2 tablespoons rice vinegar

Heat half of the oil in wok or large frying pan; stir-fry tempeh until browned, remove from wok. **Heat** remaining oil in wok; stir-fry onion and garlic until onion is soft.

Add asparagus; stir-fry until tender. Add peas and bok choy; stir-fry until bok choy is just wilted. Add sprouts, sauce, stock, mirin and vinegar; stir until sauce boils.

Return tempeh to wok; stir-fry until hot.

SERVES 4
per serving 9.6g fat; 812kJ
on the table in 30 minutes

12 pad thai

250g dried rice stick noodles

450g chicken thigh fillets, sliced thinly

1 clove garlic, crushed

1 teaspoon grated fresh ginger

2 small fresh red chillies, seeded, sliced thinly

2 tablespoons brown sugar

2 tablespoons soy sauce

1/4 cup (60ml) sweet chilli sauce

1 tablespoon fish sauce

1 tablespoon lime juice

3 green onions, sliced thinly

1 cup (80g) bean sprouts

1 cup (80g) snow pea sprouts

1/4 cup coarsely chopped fresh coriander

Place noodles in large heatproof bowl; cover with boiling water. Stand until just tender; drain.
Meanwhile, heat oiled wok or large frying pan; stir-fry chicken, garlic, ginger and chilli, in batches, until chicken is browned and cooked through.
Return chicken mixture to wok with sugar, sauces and juice; stir-fry until sauce thickens slightly. Add noodles, onion and sprouts to wok; stir-fry until hot.
Serve pad thai sprinkled with coriander.

SERVES 4
per serving 9.2g fat; 1717kJ
on the table in 30 minutes

14 fish parcels with lime coriander dressing

4 thick white fish
fillets (800g)

1 teaspoon cracked
black peppercorns

1 medium carrot
(120g), cut into
thin strips

1 small red capsicum
(150g), cut into
thin strips

2 green onions,
cut into thin strips

**lime coriander
dressing**

2 tablespoons
lime juice

1 tablespoon
soy sauce

1 teaspoon honey

½ teaspoon
sesame oil

1 clove garlic, crushed

1 tablespoon chopped
fresh coriander

Preheat oven to hot. Place each fillet on a large
sheet of baking paper or foil, sprinkle with
pepper; top with carrot, capsicum and onion.
Seal ends to enclose fish and vegetables.
Place parcels on oven tray, bake in hot oven
about 30 minutes or until fish is cooked through.
Open parcels, drain of excess liquid; drizzle
with lime coriander dressing to serve.
Lime coriander dressing Combine ingredients
in screw-topped jar; shake well.

SERVES 4
per serving 5.1g fat; 989kJ
on the table in 40 minutes

haloumi salad
on pide

280g jar antipasto char-grilled vegetables

170g jar marinated artichoke hearts

250g haloumi cheese

1/2 long loaf pide

200g baby rocket leaves

250g teardrop tomatoes

1/4 cup (60ml) balsamic vinegar

2 tablespoons pine nuts, toasted

Drain antipasto over a bowl and reserve 1/3 cup (80ml) of the oil; slice vegetables. Drain artichokes; cut into quarters.
Cut cheese into eight slices; cook in heated oiled small frying pan until browned both sides.
Meanwhile, cut bread into 1cm slices; toast under heated grill until browned both sides.
Divide toasted bread among four plates; top with rocket, antipasto, artichokes, cheese and tomatoes. Drizzle with combined reserved oil and vinegar; sprinkle with pine nuts.

SERVES 4
per serving 48.9g fat; 3051kJ
on the table in 25 minutes

lamb kebabs
with pitta and salad

500g diced lamb

1/4 cup (60ml) lemon juice

2 tablespoons olive oil

1 clove garlic, crushed

2 medium tomatoes (300g)

1/2 cup (80g) seeded black olives

200g fetta cheese

1 tablespoon olive oil, extra

8 pocket pitta

80g baby spinach leaves

Combine lamb, juice, oil and garlic in medium bowl.
Slice tomatoes thickly. Quarter olives; crumble cheese.
Thread lamb onto eight skewers; reserve marinade.
Heat extra oil in large frying pan; cook kebabs until browned all over and cooked as desired.
Pour marinade over kebabs; cook until marinade boils.
Serve kebabs on bread with spinach, tomato, olives and cheese.

SERVES 4
per serving 31.9g fat; 2832kJ
on the table in 35 minutes

18 veal scaloppine
with polenta

1 tablespoon olive oil

12 veal steaks (960g)

60g butter

1 tablespoon
lemon juice

2 tablespoons
coarsely chopped
fresh flat-leaf parsley

polenta

3 cups (750ml) water

1½ cups (375ml)
chicken stock

1 cup (170g) polenta

½ cup (125ml) milk

½ cup (40g) grated
pecorino cheese

Heat oil in large frying pan; cook veal, in batches, until browned both sides and cooked as desired. Cover to keep warm.
Melt butter in same pan, stir in juice and parsley.
Serve veal on polenta; drizzle with butter mixture.
Polenta Combine the water and stock in a large saucepan; bring to a boil. Reduce heat to a simmer; gradually whisk in polenta. Cook, uncovered, stirring occasionally, about 25 minutes or until the mixture is thickened. Stir in milk and cheese; continue stirring for 5 minutes or until the mixture is thickened.

SERVES 6
per serving 18.5g fat; 1725kJ
on the table in 40 minutes

lamb cutlets with olive
salsa, polenta and fennel

12 lamb cutlets, trimmed

1¹/₂ cups (375ml) water

2 cups (500ml) chicken stock

1 cup (170g) instant polenta

¹/₃ cup (30g) finely grated parmesan cheese

¹/₂ cup (125ml) cream

1 tablespoon olive oil

4 baby fennel, sliced thinly

100g seeded black olives, chopped coarsely

2 tablespoons lemon juice

1 clove garlic, crushed

1 tablespoon coarsely chopped fresh flat-leaf parsley

1 tablespoon olive oil, extra

Cook lamb, in batches, under hot grill until browned both sides and cooked as desired.
Meanwhile, combine the water and stock in medium saucepan. Bring to a boil, add polenta; cook, stirring, over low heat until thickened. Stir in cheese and cream.
Heat oil in medium frying pan; cook fennel, stirring, until tender.
Combine olives, juice, garlic, parsley and extra oil in medium bowl. Serve olive mixture on lamb with polenta and fennel.

SERVES 4
per serving 37.4g fat; 2654kJ
on the table in 35 minutes

20 angel hair pasta

with rocket, tomato and fetta

375g angel hair pasta

200g fetta cheese, crumbled

1/4 cup (60ml) olive oil

2 fresh red thai chillies, seeded, chopped finely

2 tablespoons shredded fresh basil

1/4 cup coarsely chopped fresh flat-leaf parsley

3 cloves garlic, crushed

3 medium tomatoes (570g), seeded, sliced thinly

250g rocket, chopped coarsely

Cook pasta in large saucepan of boiling water, uncovered, until just tender.
Meanwhile, combine half of the cheese with remaining ingredients in large bowl.
Toss drained pasta with cheese mixture. Top with remaining cheese.

SERVES 4
per serving 26.9g fat; 2516kJ
on the table in 20 minutes

thai-style **fish** cutlets

4 blue-eye cutlets (800g)

4 green onions,
sliced thinly

4 kaffir lime leaves,
shredded thinly

80g fresh ginger, peeled,
sliced thinly

1/4 cup coarsely chopped
fresh coriander

1 tablespoon brown sugar

2 tablespoons sweet
chilli sauce

2 teaspoons peanut oil

1 teaspoon fish sauce

2 tablespoons lime juice

Preheat oven to moderate. Place cutlets
on large individual pieces of foil; top each
cutlet with equal amounts of onion, lime leaf,
ginger, coriander and sugar. Drizzle combined
remaining ingredients over each serving
then fold foil over the top, pinching it tightly
to enclose cutlets.
Place fish parcels on oven tray; cook in
moderate oven 20 minutes then test one
parcel to see if fish is cooked as desired.
Fish parcels can also be placed on preheated
grill of covered barbecue and cooked about
10 minutes or until fish is cooked as desired.

SERVES 4
per serving 7.2g fat; 1171kJ
on the table in 30 minutes

700g pork fillets

750g kumara, sliced thickly

1 tablespoon seeded mustard

2 tablespoons honey

1 tablespoon soy sauce

4 green onions, sliced thinly

Preheat oven to very hot.

Place pork and kumara in oiled baking dish with combined mustard, honey and sauce; toss to coat pork and kumara in honey mixture.

Cook undrained pork and kumara, uncovered, in very hot oven about 30 minutes or until pork is cooked through and kumara is tender.

Slice pork; serve with kumara and green onion, drizzle with pan juices. Accompany with steamed sugar snap peas, if desired.

SERVES 4
per serving 4.4g fat; 1505kJ
on the table in 40 minutes

beef and crunchy
noodle salad

600g beef rump steak

400g baby bok choy, shredded

3 green onions, sliced

1 cup (80g) bean sprouts

50g shiitake mushrooms, sliced thinly

2 tablespoons fresh coriander leaves

250g cherry tomatoes, halved

1/3 cup (80ml) soy sauce

1 teaspoon sesame oil

2 tablespoons sherry

100g packet crunchy noodles

Cook beef on heated oiled grill plate (or non-stick pan or under grill) until browned both sides and cooked as desired. Stand 5 minutes; slice thinly.
Meanwhile, combine bok choy, onion, sprouts, mushrooms, coriander and tomato in large bowl.
Combine sauce, oil and sherry in screw-topped jar; shake well.
Add beef, dressing and noodles to bok choy mixture; toss gently to combine.

SERVES 4
per serving 11.5g fat; 1277kJ
on the table in 25 minutes

salmon fillets with
red capsicum butter

1 small red capsicum (150g), halved, seeded

1 tablespoon olive oil

1 tablespoon coarse cooking salt

6 medium salmon fillets (1.2kg), skin on

125g butter

1 clove garlic, crushed

1 fresh red thai chilli, seeded, chopped finely

1 tablespoon lime juice

2 tablespoons chopped fresh coriander

Roast capsicum, skin-side up, under grill or in very hot oven until skin blisters and blackens. Cover capsicum with plastic or paper for 5 minutes, then peel away skin; chop flesh finely. Rub combined oil and salt onto salmon skin; place salmon, skin-side up, on oiled oven tray. Cook under hot grill about 8 minutes or until skin is browned and crisp.
Meanwhile, melt butter in small saucepan, add garlic and chilli; cook, stirring, until fragrant. Add capsicum, juice and coriander; cook, stirring, until hot. Serve salmon with red capsicum butter.

SERVES 6
per serving 34.4g fat; 1959kJ
on the table in 40 minutes

fish fillets with coriander
chilli sauce

12 x 70g ocean
perch fillets

1 medium brown
onion (150g),
sliced thinly

1 cup (250ml) water

*1/2 cup (125ml)
dry vermouth*

*1/3 cup (80ml)
lime juice*

2 fresh red thai
chillies, seeded,
chopped finely

1/3 cup (75g) sugar

2 teaspoons
cornflour

2 tablespoons finely
chopped fresh
coriander

1 medium red
capsicum (200g),
sliced thinly

4 green onions, cut
into 5cm lengths

*1/2 cup firmly
packed fresh
coriander leaves*

Preheat oven to moderate. Place fish in single layer
in shallow ovenproof dish; top with brown onion.
Pour over combined water, vermouth and half of
the juice; cover. Bake in moderate oven about
15 minutes or until fish is cooked as desired.
Remove fish; keep warm. Strain and reserve liquid.
Place reserved liquid, chilli, sugar and combined
cornflour and remaining juice in small saucepan.
Stir over heat until sugar dissolves; bring to
a boil. Reduce heat; simmer until mixture thickens.
Stir in chopped coriander.
Arrange fish, capsicum, green onion and coriander
leaves on serving plate; drizzle with sauce.

SERVES 4
per serving 1.5g fat; 1237kJ
on the table in 35 minutes

28 chicken with

mustard and sun-dried tomato sauce

30g butter

1 clove garlic, crushed

4 single chicken breast fillets (680g)

3/4 cup (180ml) chicken stock

1 tablespoon seeded mustard

1/4 cup (35g) drained sun-dried tomatoes, chopped finely

4 green onions, chopped finely

Heat butter in large frying pan; cook garlic, stirring, 1 minute. Add chicken; cook until browned both sides and cooked through. Remove chicken from pan.
Add stock to same pan; bring to a boil, stirring. Reduce heat; simmer, uncovered, 5 minutes. Stir in mustard, tomato and onion.
Serve sliced chicken drizzled with sauce; accompany with roasted potato slices, if desired.

SERVES 4
per serving 16.5g fat; 1250kJ
on the table in 25 minutes

30 warm lamb salad with
sun-dried tomatoes

500g lamb fillets

1 clove garlic, crushed

1/4 cup (60ml) balsamic vinegar

1/3 cup (80ml) olive oil

1/3 cup (50g) drained sun-dried tomatoes, sliced thickly

15g butter

250g fresh asparagus, chopped coarsely

1 medium red capsicum (200g), chopped coarsely

150g button mushrooms, quartered

80g baby rocket

Cook lamb in heated large non-stick frying pan until browned and cooked as desired; slice lamb. Combine lamb, garlic, vinegar, oil and tomato in large bowl.

Heat butter in same pan; cook asparagus, capsicum and mushrooms, stirring, until asparagus is tender.

Combine asparagus mixture, lamb mixture and rocket in large bowl; toss gently.

SERVES 4
per serving 29.8g fat; 1753kJ
on the table in 35 minutes

lemon chicken with
garlic potatoes

1 medium
lemon (140g)

2 teaspoons chopped
fresh thyme

2 tablespoons honey

2 tablespoons olive oil

4 single chicken
breast fillets (680g)

8 baby new
potatoes (320g)

20g butter

2 cloves garlic, crushed

4 sprigs fresh thyme

Peel rind thinly from half of the lemon, avoiding white pith. Cut rind into thin strips. Squeeze lemon; you need ¼ cup (60ml) lemon juice.
Combine rind, juice, chopped thyme, honey and half of the oil in shallow bowl; add chicken, coat all over with marinade.
Boil, steam or microwave potatoes until tender; drain. Heat butter in small frying pan, add garlic and potatoes; stir until potatoes are coated in butter mixture.
Meanwhile, drain chicken; reserve marinade. Heat remaining oil in large frying pan; add chicken, cook over medium heat until browned both sides. Add thyme sprigs and reserved marinade; simmer, covered, until chicken is cooked through. Serve chicken, topped with thyme mixture, with slices of potato and steamed beans, if desired.

SERVES 4
per serving 22.7g fat; 1881kJ
on the table in 35 minutes

40g piece fresh ginger

*4 small whole
snapper (1.2kg)*

*¼ cup (60ml)
vegetable stock*

*4 green onions,
sliced thinly*

*½ cup firmly packed
fresh coriander leaves*

*⅓ cup (80ml) salt-
reduced light
soy sauce*

1 teaspoon sesame oil

Peel ginger; cut into thin strips lengthways, then cut into matchstick-sized pieces.

Score fish three times on each side; place each fish on a separate large sheet of foil. Sprinkle with ginger, then drizzle with half of the stock; fold foil loosely to enclose fish.

Place fish in large bamboo steamer; steam fish, covered, over wok or large frying pan of simmering water about 30 minutes or until cooked through.

Transfer fish to serving dish; sprinkle with onion and coriander, then drizzle with combined remaining stock, sauce and oil. Serve with steamed broccoli and baby corn, if desired.

SERVES 4
per serving 3.2g fat; 573kJ
on the table in 40 minutes

chicken, coriander
and cashew stir-fry

700g chicken breast fillets, sliced thinly

1/4 cup coarsely chopped fresh coriander

2 fresh red thai chillies, seeded, chopped finely

1 teaspoon sesame oil

2 cloves garlic, crushed

2 teaspoons peanut oil

1/3 cup (80ml) rice vinegar

1/4 cup (60ml) sweet chilli sauce

1 tablespoon lime juice

1/4 cup (35g) raw cashews, toasted

2/3 cup (40g) snow pea sprouts

2/3 cup (40g) snow pea tendrils

Combine chicken, coriander, chilli, sesame oil and garlic in large bowl.
Heat peanut oil in wok or large frying pan; stir-fry chicken mixture, in batches, until browned and cooked through.
Return chicken mixture to wok. Add vinegar, sauce and juice; stir-fry until sauce boils. Add cashews; stir-fry until just combined.
Remove wok from heat, toss through sprouts and tendrils.

SERVES 4
per serving 18g fat; 1539kJ
on the table in 35 minutes

chermoulla lamb

with tabbouleh

*660g lamb backstraps
(eye of loin), sliced thinly*

*1/2 cup coarsely chopped
fresh flat-leaf parsley*

1 tablespoon lemon rind

2 tablespoons lemon juice

*1 tablespoon
ground cumin*

*1 tablespoon
ground coriander*

*2 teaspoons
ground turmeric*

*1/4 teaspoon
cayenne pepper*

*1 medium red onion
(170g), chopped finely*

tabbouleh

1/3 cup (55g) burghul

*3 cups coarsely chopped
fresh flat-leaf parsley*

*1/4 cup coarsely chopped
fresh mint*

*3 medium tomatoes
(570g), chopped*

*2 green onions,
chopped finely*

*1/3 cup (80ml)
chicken stock*

1/3 cup (80ml) lemon juice

Combine ingredients in large bowl.
Heat oiled wok or large frying pan; stir-fry
lamb mixture, in batches, until browned and
cooked as desired. Serve with tabbouleh.
Tabbouleh Cover burghul with cold water,
stand 15 minutes. Drain; press as much
water as possible from burghul. Place
burghul in large bowl. Add remaining
ingredients; mix well.

SERVES 4
per serving 7g fat; 1215kJ
on the table in 35 minutes

cajun chicken with tomato salsa

750g chicken breast fillets, sliced thinly

¼ cup cajun seasoning

2 teaspoons grated lime rind

2 trimmed corn cobs (500g)

2 tablespoons olive oil

1 small red onion (100g), cut into thin wedges

tomato salsa

2 small egg tomatoes (120g), chopped finely

2 green onions, sliced thinly

2 teaspoons lime juice

2 teaspoons balsamic vinegar

Combine chicken, seasoning and rind in large bowl; mix well. Cut kernels from corn.
Heat half of the oil in wok or large frying pan; stir-fry chicken mixture, in batches, until cooked through.
Heat remaining oil in wok; stir-fry corn and onion until onion is soft.
Return chicken to wok; stir-fry until hot. Serve chicken mixture topped with tomato salsa.
Tomato salsa Combine ingredients in small bowl; mix well.

SERVES 4
per serving 16g fat; 1740kJ
on the table in 35 minutes

38 mustard rosemary
chicken

2 tablespoons
lemon juice

2 tablespoons olive oil

2 cloves garlic,
crushed

2 tablespoons finely
chopped fresh
rosemary

1/4 cup (60g)
seeded mustard

1kg chicken
thigh fillets

1/2 cup (125ml) dry
white wine

300ml cream

1 teaspoon cornflour

1 teaspoon water

1 tablespoon finely
chopped fresh
rosemary, extra

Combine juice, oil, garlic, rosemary, mustard
and chicken in medium bowl; stir until chicken
is well coated in mixture.
Drain chicken over small bowl; reserve liquid.
Cook chicken on heated oiled grill plate (or grill
or barbecue) until browned and cooked through.
Place reserved liquid and wine in small
saucepan, bring to a boil; simmer until reduced
by half. Stir in cream, then blended cornflour
and water; bring to a boil, stirring until mixture
thickens slightly. Serve chicken with sauce;
sprinkle with extra rosemary.

SERVES 4
per serving 60.4g fat; 3222kJ
on the table in 25 minutes

and vietnamese mint

1 tablespoon
peanut oil

500g beef eye fillet

1 clove garlic, crushed

1 tablespoon finely
shredded fresh ginger

2 fresh red thai
chillies, seeded,
sliced finely

1/4 cup (60ml)
lime juice

1/4 cup (60ml) water

2 tablespoons
soy sauce

1 tablespoon sugar

2 tablespoons finely
chopped fresh
vietnamese mint

Preheat oven to moderate. Heat oil in large non-stick frying pan; cook beef until browned all over.
Transfer beef to baking tray; roast, uncovered, in moderate oven 10 minutes for rare or until cooked as desired. Stand 10 minutes; slice beef.
Add garlic, ginger and chilli to pan juices; stir over heat 1 minute. Add juice, the water, sauce and sugar; bring to a boil. Remove from heat, stir in mint. Pour mixture over sliced beef to serve.

SERVES 4
per serving 10.6g fat; 946kJ
on the table in 30 minutes

curried lamb cutlets
with tomato chickpea salad

12 lamb cutlets, trimmed

2 tablespoons yogurt

1 clove garlic

1 teaspoon garam masala

½ teaspoon ground cumin

¼ teaspoon chilli powder

lemon yogurt sauce

³/₄ cup (210g) yogurt

1 tablespoon lemon juice

1 tablespoon water

1 teaspoon ground cumin

1 clove garlic, crushed

1 tablespoon finely
chopped fresh coriander

tomato chickpea salad

2 x 300g cans chickpeas,
rinsed, drained

2 medium tomatoes (380g),
seeded, chopped

1 medium red onion (170g),
chopped finely

1 tablespoon olive oil

2 tablespoons lemon juice

2 teaspoons finely chopped
fresh coriander

2 cloves garlic, crushed

Toss lamb in large bowl
with combined yogurt, garlic
and spices.
Cook lamb on heated oiled
grill plate (or grill or barbecue)
until browned both sides and
cooked as desired.
Serve drizzled with lemon
yogurt sauce, accompanied
by tomato chickpea salad.
Lemon yogurt sauce
Whisk ingredients together
in small bowl.
Tomato chickpea salad
Combine ingredients in
medium bowl.

SERVES 4
per serving 19.6g fat; 1715kJ
on the table in 35 minutes

seasoned tuna steaks
with tomato salsa

4 tuna steaks (800g)

1 tablespoon cajun
seasoning

100g baby spinach

2 medium tomatoes
(380g), seeded,
diced finely

1 tablespoon coarsely
chopped fresh mint

1 tablespoon
lemon juice

Sprinkle tuna with cajun seasoning. Cook tuna
on heated oiled grill plate (or grill or barbecue)
until browned both sides and cooked as desired.
Serve tuna on spinach; top with combined
tomato, mint and juice.

SERVES 4
per serving 11.6g fat; 1342kJ
on the table in 20 minutes

chicken broth

with rice noodles

*1.5 litres (6 cups)
chicken stock*

2 cups (500ml) water

*50g piece fresh
ginger, sliced thinly*

*350g chicken
breast fillets*

*500g fresh flat
rice noodles*

*1/4 cup (60ml)
lime juice*

*1 tablespoon
fish sauce*

*4 green onions,
chopped coarsely*

*2 fresh red thai
chillies, seeded,
sliced thinly*

*2 tablespoons
coarsely chopped
fresh coriander*

*1 cup (80g)
bean sprouts*

Bring stock, the water and ginger to a boil in large saucepan. Add chicken; return to a boil. Reduce heat; simmer, covered, about 15 minutes or until chicken is cooked through. Remove chicken; cool 5 minutes then shred coarsely.
Meanwhile, return broth mixture to a boil; add noodles, juice and sauce. Separate noodles with fork, add chicken and remaining ingredients to broth; stir gently over heat until hot.

SERVES 4
per serving 7.4g fat; 1711kJ
on the table in 35 minutes

fish with chermoulla

1kg snapper fillet

3 cloves garlic, crushed

1 teaspoon ground cumin

1/2 teaspoon hot paprika

2 tablespoons coarsely chopped
fresh coriander

2 tablespoons coarsely chopped
fresh flat-leaf parsley

1/4 cup (60ml) olive oil

2 teaspoons finely grated lemon rind

1/4 cup (60ml) lemon juice

Cut fish into eight even-sized pieces.
Place in large shallow dish.
Combine remaining ingredients in medium
bowl. Pour half of the chermoulla over fish.
Cook fish, in batches, in heated oiled
non-stick frying pan until browned both
sides and cooked through.
Serve fish drizzled with remaining
chermoulla; sprinkle with extra coriander
leaves, if desired.

SERVES 4
per serving 17.8g fat; 1559kJ
on the table in 25 minutes

tandoori beef with
grilled limes

4 beef rib-eye
(scotch fillet)
steaks (600g)

1 clove garlic, crushed

1/4 cup (75g)
tandoori paste

4 limes, halved

1/2 cup (175g)
mango chutney

3/4 cup (210g) yogurt

2 tablespoons
finely chopped
fresh coriander

Combine beef, garlic and paste in large bowl;
stand 10 minutes.

Cook beef on heated oiled grill plate (or grill
or barbecue) about 10 minutes or until browned
both sides and cooked as desired.

Meanwhile, add lime to grill plate; cook about
2 minutes or until browned.

Serve beef with lime halves, mango chutney, and
combined yogurt and coriander. Accompany
with steamed green beans, if desired.

SERVES 4
per serving 16.9g fat; 1669kJ
on the table in 30 minutes

asian lamb salad

with lime dressing

660g lamb backstraps
(eye of loin)

1 medium carrot (120g)

1 lebanese
cucumber (130g)

1 small chinese
cabbage (350g),
shredded coarsely

2 cups (160g)
bean sprouts

3 green onions,
sliced thinly

2 small red radishes,
sliced thinly

1/4 cup (35g) roasted
unsalted peanuts,
chopped coarsely

lime dressing

1 tablespoon
rice vinegar

1/4 cup (60ml)
lime juice

1 clove garlic, crushed

1 tablespoon sugar

1/4 cup (60ml)
fish sauce

1 small fresh red
chilli, seeded,
chopped finely

Cook lamb on heated oiled grill plate (or grill
or barbecue) until browned both sides and
cooked as desired. Remove from pan; stand,
covered, 15 minutes.

Meanwhile, using vegetable peeler, slice
carrot and cucumber lengthways into ribbons.
Combine cabbage, carrot, cucumber, sprouts,
onion and radish in large bowl.

Slice lamb thinly. Pour lime dressing over
salad; toss gently to combine. Top salad
with lamb; sprinkle with peanuts.

Lime dressing Combine ingredients in small jug.

SERVES 4
per serving 10.5g fat; 1238kJ
on the table in 30 minutes

beef and
noodle stir-fry

250g rice stick noodles

1 tablespoon peanut oil

500g beef eye fillet, sliced thinly

1 clove garlic, crushed

1 tablespoon finely chopped fresh lemon grass

2 fresh red thai chillies, seeded, sliced thinly

1/3 cup (80ml) lime juice

1 tablespoon fish sauce

100g baby rocket

1 cup (80g) bean sprouts

1/2 cup loosely packed fresh coriander leaves

1/2 cup loosely packed fresh mint leaves

3 green onions, sliced thinly

1 lebanese cucumber (130g), seeded, sliced thinly

Place noodles in large heatproof bowl, cover with boiling water; stand 5 minutes or until tender, drain.

Meanwhile, heat half of the oil in wok or large frying pan; cook beef, in batches, until browned.

Heat remaining oil in wok; cook garlic, lemon grass and chilli until fragrant. Return beef to wok with juice and sauce; stir-fry until heated through.

Add noodles; stir-fry until combined. Stir in remaining ingredients; serve immediately.

SERVES 4
per serving 11.7g fat; 1720kJ
on the table in 35 minutes

garden herbs and roast tomato

*4 single chicken
breast fillets (680g)*

*¼ cup finely chopped
fresh chives*

*¼ cup finely chopped
fresh oregano*

*2 cloves garlic,
crushed*

*1 tablespoon
chicken stock*

500g cherry tomatoes

*⅓ cup (80ml) sweet
chilli sauce*

*250g fresh asparagus
spears, trimmed*

Preheat oven to moderate. Combine chicken, herbs,
garlic and stock in large bowl.
Cook chicken in large oiled non-stick frying pan until
browned. Place chicken in a shallow baking dish with
combined tomatoes and sauce. Bake, uncovered, in moderate
oven for 15 minutes or until chicken is cooked through.
Meanwhile, boil, steam or microwave asparagus until just
tender. Serve chicken with tomatoes and asparagus.

SERVES 4
per serving 10.2g fat; 1168kJ
on the table in 35 minutes

trout with caramelised
tomatoes and balsamic

*4 medium egg
tomatoes (600g),
quartered lengthways*

1 tablespoon olive oil

2 teaspoons sugar

1 clove garlic, crushed

*4 ocean trout
cutlets (400g)*

*2 tablespoons
balsamic vinegar*

*¼ cup shredded
fresh basil leaves*

Combine tomato, oil, sugar and garlic in medium bowl.
Cook trout in heated oiled large frying pan until
browned both sides and cooked through.
Wipe pan with absorbent paper, add tomato mixture; cook,
stirring, over high heat until softened and lightly browned.
Serve fish with tomato, drizzled with vinegar and
sprinkled with basil.

SERVES 4
per serving 8.2g fat; 715kJ
on the table in 25 minutes

honeyed garlic
lamb and
vegetable stir-fry

2 tablespoons
peanut oil

400g lamb fillets,
sliced thinly

1 clove garlic, crushed

3 baby eggplants
(180g), sliced thinly

1 medium white onion
(150g), sliced thinly

1 medium carrot
(120g), sliced thinly

1 medium red
capsicum (200g),
sliced thinly

425g can baby
corn, drained

100g snow peas

1 tablespoon cornflour

2 tablespoons
oyster sauce

1 tablespoon
soy sauce

1 tablespoon honey

Heat half of the oil in wok or large frying pan; stir-fry lamb and garlic, in batches, until lamb is browned.

Heat remaining oil in wok; stir-fry eggplant and onion until just softened.

Add carrot and capsicum; stir-fry until vegetables are just tender. Add corn and snow peas; stir-fry, tossing to combine.

Return lamb mixture to wok with blended cornflour, sauces and honey; stir until mixture boils and thickens slightly.

SERVES 4
per serving 13.8g fat; 1442kJ
on the table in 35 minutes

mussels with garlic
and tomato sauce

1.5kg black mussels

1 cup (250ml) water

2 tablespoons coarsely chopped fresh flat-leaf parsley

garlic and tomato sauce

2 tablespoons olive oil

1 medium white onion (150g), chopped finely

6 cloves garlic, crushed

1 medium green capsicum (200g), chopped finely

100g button mushrooms, chopped coarsely

400g can tomatoes

425g can tomato puree

Scrub mussels; remove beards. Heat the water in large saucepan; cook mussels, covered, over high heat about 5 minutes or until mussels open. Discard any mussels that do not open.
Strain mussels, reserving 1 cup (250ml) of the cooking liquid to use in the sauce.
Stir mussels into garlic and tomato sauce. Serve sprinkled with parsley; accompany with crusty bread, if desired.
Garlic and tomato sauce Heat oil in large frying pan; cook onion and garlic, stirring, until onion is soft. Add capsicum and mushrooms; cook, stirring, until vegetables are soft. Stir in undrained crushed tomatoes, puree and reserved mussel cooking liquid; bring to a boil. Reduce heat; simmer, uncovered, until sauce thickens slightly.

SERVES 4
per serving 11.1g fat; 929kJ
on the table in 45 minutes

2 teaspoons grated fresh ginger

2 cloves garlic, crushed

1 tablespoon finely chopped fresh lemon grass

¼ cup (60ml) sweet chilli sauce

¼ cup (60ml) lime juice

¾ cup coarsely chopped fresh coriander

4 single chicken breast fillets (680g)

2 cups (400g) long-grain white rice

¾ cup (180ml) chicken stock

2 teaspoons cornflour

Combine ginger, garlic, lemon grass,
sauce, juice and a third of the coriander
with chicken in large bowl.
Boil, steam or microwave rice until just
tender; drain, if necessary, then stir in
remaining coriander.
Meanwhile, drain chicken over large bowl;
reserve marinade. Cook chicken in large
oiled frying pan until browned both sides
and cooked through; slice chicken thickly.
Blend 2 tablespoons of the stock with cornflour
in small jug until smooth. Combine remaining
stock, cornflour mixture and reserved marinade
in medium saucepan, stir until sauce boils
and thickens slightly.
Serve chicken on rice; drizzle with sauce.

SERVES 4
per serving 5.1g fat; 2436kJ
on the table in 30 minutes

Sprinkle fresh berries with Grand Marnier, then stir over high heat in frying pan for 1 minute. Serve hot berries with vanilla ice-cream.

Place orange slices on oven tray, sprinkle with brown sugar and Cointreau; grill until caramelised, serve with vanilla yogurt.

Serve scoops of vanilla ice-cream in a mixture of hot espresso coffee and a little Frangelico. Serve with biscotti.

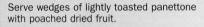

Serve wedges of lightly toasted panettone with poached dried fruit.

Stir chopped almond nougat and a couple of tablespoons of maple syrup through softened vanilla ice-cream.

Sprinkle brown sugar over cut side of peach halves; grill until golden. Scrape the seeds of one vanilla bean into double cream to serve.

Combine grated lime rind, lime juice and caster sugar with mascarpone cheese; serve with fresh mango slices.

Combine melted Toblerone and cream; serve hot sauce in individual glasses with dippers of almond biscotti.

glossary

baked ricotta baked fresh ricotta cheese; egg whites, paprika and oil are often added.

bok choy also known as bak choy, pak choy and chinese white cabbage; has a mild mustard taste. Use stems and leaves. Baby bok choy is smaller and more tender.

burghul also known as bulghur wheat; hulled, steamed wheat kernels that are dried then crushed into various-sized grains.

butter use salted or unsalted ("sweet") butter; 125g is equal to one stick of butter.

capers piquant, grey-green buds of a shrub; sold dried and salted, or pickled. Before use: if salted, rinse and drain; if pickled, drain.

capsicum also known as bell pepper or, simply, pepper. Discard membranes and seeds before use.

chilli available in many different types and sizes. Use rubber gloves when seeding and chopping fresh chillies as they can burn your skin. Removing seeds and membranes lessens the heat level.

sweet chilli sauce: a mild, Thai-style sauce made from red chillies, sugar, garlic and vinegar.

chinese cabbage also known as peking or napa cabbage, or wong bok; an elongated cabbage with pale-green, crinkly leaves.

cointreau citrus-flavoured liqueur.

cornflour also known as cornstarch; used as a thickening agent.

crème fraîche fermented cream that has a slightly tangy, nutty flavour and velvety rich texture.

eggplant also known as aubergine.

fennel also known as finocchio or anise.

fish sauce also called nam pla or nuoc nam; made from pulverised salted fermented fish, most often anchovies. Has a pungent smell and strong taste; use sparingly.

frangelico a hazelnut-flavoured liqueur.

ginger also known as green or root ginger. pickled: paper-thin shavings of pickled pink ginger.

grand marnier orange-flavoured liqueur.

haloumi firm sheep-milk cheese matured in brine; can be briefly grilled or fried without breaking down.

hoisin sauce a thick, sweet, spicy Chinese paste made from salted, fermented soy beans, onions and garlic.

kaffir lime leaves aromatic leaves of small citrus tree.

kecap manis thick soy sauce with added sugar and spice.

kumara orange-fleshed sweet potato.

lemon grass a tall, lemon-tasting and -smelling sharp-edged grass; use the white lower part of the stem.

noodles

crunchy: ready-to-eat, cooked crispy egg noodles.

fresh rice: soft white noodles made from rice flour and vegetable oil. Rinse under hot water to remove starch and excess oil before using.

hokkien: also known as stir-fry noodles; fresh wheat-flour yellow-brown noodles. Must be rinsed under hot water to remove starch and excess oil before use.

rice stick: a dried noodle, available flat and wide or very thin; made from rice flour and water.

oil

peanut: pressed from ground peanuts; has high smoke point.

sesame: made from white sesame seeds; a flavouring rather than cooking medium.

onion

green: also known as scallion or (incorrectly) shallot; an onion picked before bulb has formed, having a long, bright-green edible stalk.

red: also known as Spanish, red Spanish or Bermuda onion; a sweet-flavoured, large, purple-red onion.

oyster sauce rich, brown sauce made from oysters and brine, cooked with salt and soy sauce, and thickened with starches.

panettone light Italian yeast cake with sultanas and candied peel.

pecorino cheese hard, dry cheese with sharp, pungent taste.

pide also known as turkish bread; comes in long (about 45cm) flat loaves as well as individual rounds; made from wheat flour and sprinkled with sesame or black onion seeds.

pocket pitta wheat-flour Lebanese bread sold in flat pieces; made up of two rounds that form a pocket.

polenta flour-like cereal made of ground corn (maize); similar to cornmeal but finer and lighter in colour. Instant polenta cooks faster than regular polenta.

prosciutto salt-cured, air-dried, pressed ham, usually sold in paper-thin ready-to-eat pieces.

rice vinegar colourless vinegar made from fermented rice, and flavoured with sugar and salt.

rocket also known as arugula, rugula and rucola; a peppery-tasting green leaf which can be used similarly to baby spinach leaves, eaten raw in salads or used in cooking. Baby rocket leaves are both smaller and less peppery.

shiitake mushrooms mushroom with elongated golden-brown cap and a unique meaty flavour.

sprouts tender new growths of assorted beans and seeds. The most readily available are mung bean, soy bean, alfalfa and snow pea sprouts.

snow pea tendrils growing shoots of snow pea plant; sold by greengrocers.

spinach also known as English spinach and incorrectly, silverbeet.

tempeh produced by natural culture of soy beans; has a chunky, chewy texture.

toblerone chocolate bar; purchase in supermarkets.

vanilla bean dried, long, thin pod that contains tiny black seeds that taste of vanilla.

vietnamese mint narrow-leafed pungent herb, also known as cambodian mint, daun laksa and laksa leaf.

vermouth, dry a wine flavoured with a variety of herbs; mostly used as an aperitif and for cocktails.

watercress vegetable with small, rounded, deep-green leaves and a slightly bitter, peppery flavour.

index

These conversions are approximate only, but the difference between an exact and the approximate conversion of various liquid and dry measures is minimal and will not affect your cooking results.

Measuring equipment

The difference between one country's measuring cups and another's is, at most, within a 2 or 3 teaspoon variance. (For the record, 1 Australian metric measuring cup holds approximately 250ml.) The most accurate way of measuring dry ingredients is to weigh them. For liquids, use a clear glass or plastic jug having metric markings.

Note: NZ, Canada, USA and UK all use 15ml tablespoons. Australian tablespoons measure 20ml.

All cup and spoon measurements are level.

How to measure

When using graduated measuring cups, shake dry ingredients loosely into the appropriate cup. Do not tap the cup on a bench or tightly pack the ingredients unless directed to do so. Level the top of measuring cups and measuring spoons with a knife. When measuring liquids, place a clear glass or plastic jug having metric markings on a flat surface to check accuracy at eye level.

Dry Measures

metric	imperial
15g	1/2oz
30g	1oz
60g	2oz
90g	3oz
125g	4oz (1/4lb)
155g	5oz
185g	6oz
220g	7oz
250g	8oz (1/2lb)
280g	9oz
315g	10oz
345g	11oz
375g	12oz (3/4lb)
410g	13oz
440g	14oz
470g	15oz
500g	16oz (1lb)
750g	24oz (1 1/2lb)
1kg	32oz (2lb)

We use large eggs having an average weight of 60g.

Liquid Measures

metric	imperial
30ml	1 fluid oz
60ml	2 fluid oz
100ml	3 fluid oz
125ml	4 fluid oz
150ml	5 fluid oz (1/4 pint/1 gill)
190ml	6 fluid oz
250ml (1cup)	8 fluid oz
300ml	10 fluid oz (1/2 pint)
500ml	16 fluid oz
600ml	20 fluid oz (1 pint)
1000ml (1litre)	1 3/4 pints

Helpful Measures

metric	imperial
3mm	1/8in
6mm	1/4in
1cm	1/2in
2cm	3/4in
2.5cm	1in
6cm	2 1/2in
8cm	3in
20cm	8in
23cm	9in
25cm	10in
30cm	12in (1ft)

Oven Temperatures

These oven temperatures are only a guide.
Always check the manufacturer's manual.

	°C (Celsius)	°F (Fahrenheit)	Gas Mark
Very slow	120	250	1
Slow	150	300	2
Moderately slow	160	325	3
Moderate	180 –190	350 – 375	4
Moderately hot	200 – 210	400 – 425	5
Hot	220 – 230	450 – 475	6
Very hot	240 – 250	500 – 525	7

at your fingertips

These elegant slipcovers store up to 10 mini books and make the books instantly accessible.

And the metric measuring cups and spoons make following our recipes a piece of cake.

Book Holder
Australia and overseas:
$8.95 (incl. GST).

Metric Measuring Set
Australia: $6.50 (incl. GST).
New Zealand: $8.00.
Elsewhere: $9.95.
Prices include postage
and handling.
This offer is available
in all countries.

Photocopy and complete the coupon below

Mail or fax Photocopy and complete the coupon below and post to ACP Books Reader Offer, ACP Publishing, GPO Box 4967, Sydney NSW 2001, *or* fax to (02) 9267 4967.

Phone Have your credit card details ready, then phone 136 116 (Mon-Fri, 8.00am - 6.00pm; Sat 8.00am - 6.00pm).

Australian residents We accept the credit cards listed on the coupon, money orders and cheques.

Overseas residents We accept the credit cards listed on the coupon, drafts in $A drawn on an Australian bank, and also British, New Zealand and U.S. cheques in the currency of the country of issue.

☐ **Book holder**   ☐ **Metric measuring set**
Please indicate number(s) required.

Mr/Mrs/Ms _____

Address _____

_____

Postcode _____ Country _____

Phone: Business hours ( ) _____

I enclose my cheque/money order for $_____ payable to ACP Publishing

OR: please charge $ _____ to my: ☐ Bankcard ☐ Visa

☐ Amex ☐ MasterCard ☐ Diners Club   Expiry Date ___/___

Cardholder's signature _____

Please allow up to 30 days for delivery within Australia.

Allow up to 6 weeks for overseas deliveries. Both offers expire 31/12/02.
HLMFF02

Food director Pamela Clark
Food editor Louise Patniotis

ACP BOOKS STAFF
Editorial director Susan Tomnay
Senior editor Julie Collard
Concept design Jackie Richards
Designer Caryl Wiggins
Publishing manager (sales) Jennifer McDon
Publishing manager (rights & new titles)
Jane Hazell
Assistant brand manager Donna Gianniotis
Production manager Carol Currie

Publisher Sue Wannan
Group publisher Jill Baker
Chief executive officer John Alexander

Produced by ACP Books, Sydney.

Colour separations by
ACP Colour Graphics Pty Ltd, Sydney.
Printing by Dai Nippon Printing in Hong Kong

Published by ACP Publishing Pty Limited,
54 Park St, Sydney; GPO Box 4088, Sydney,
NSW 1028. Ph: (02) 9282 8618
Fax: (02) 9267 9438.
acpbooks@acp.com.au
www.acpbooks.com.au

To order books, phone 136 116.
Send recipe enquiries to
Recipeenquiries@acp.com.au

Australia Distributed by Network Services,
GPO Box 4088, Sydney, NSW 1028.
Ph: (02) 9282 8777 Fax: (02) 9264 3278.

United Kingdom Distributed by Australian
Consolidated Press (UK), Moulton Park Busin
Centre, Red House Road, Moulton Park,
Northampton, NN3 6AQ. Ph: (01604) 497 531
Fax: (01604) 497 533 acpukltd@aol.com

Canada Distributed by Whitecap Books Ltd,
351 Lynn Ave, North Vancouver, BC, V7J 2C4
Ph: (604) 980 9852.

New Zealand Distributed by Netlink Distributio
Company, Level 4, 23 Hargreaves St,
College Hill, Auckland 1, Ph: (9) 302 7616.

South Africa Distributed by
PSD Promotions (Pty) Ltd, PO Box 1175,
Isando 1600, SA, Ph: (011) 392 6065.

Clark, Pamela.
Fast food for friends.

Includes index.
ISBN 186396 275 1

1. Entertaining. 2. Quick and easy cookery
3. Cookery. I. Title: Australian Women's Weekly
(Series: Australian Women's Weekly Make it
Tonight mini series).

641.568

© ACP Publishing Pty Limited 2002
ABN 18 053 273 546

Cover: Asian lamb salad with lime
dressing, page 47.
Stylist: Andrew Birley
Photographer: Alan Benson
Back cover: Lamb cutlets with olive salsa,
polenta and fennel, page 19.